How to Love a Wildflower
Chloe Camille Seymour

To: you, those who slung me onto their backs for as long as they could, our city and the unceasing possibility of blooming.

"If you have to explain Detroit to someone, they will never understand it."

*I went from unmedicated to medicated to unmedicated while writing this. There are inconsistencies in my tense and my style, my understanding of my own fragility and my ability to process the strength I've uncovered on my own.

There are two consistencies - I loved you. I love Detroit.

**This is a compilation of finding tags, touches and tarnishes you left on my body and discovering a way to piece them all together.

***

Mental illness is hilarious.

To me.

No one else's. Just mine.

When I am in the middle of a lull, I have an inability to explain my brain and its patterns that is so remarkably frustrating — I usually backtrack and hem and haw and laugh and resort to "it's fine though, how have you been?" — it is my most refined defense.

When I am in the depths of it I can't verbalize how I have been panicking since I was seven years old — even then I was thinking about how the sky was too big or how death was inevitable or how the doorway to the attic was in my room and was an open opportunity for intruders to kidnap me from my bed. Throughout adolescence I had to have my parents tell me "all living things pass" before bedtime so I could sleep. They either thought I was going to be a sociopath or a genius with the means to understand the universe's innerworkings. They got a mass of excess empathy. That's a nice happy medium.

"When did you first start to feel that way?"

That's the knee-jerk question when people first find out you're depressed/full of panic/anxiety-ridden-enough-to-be-medicated. It is a combination of not knowing if it's okay to ask whether I'm functional without offending me while indicating they also have questioned their own disposition at some point.

"It doesn't start with just one day."

That's about as far as I get before I fumble the ball.

And after years of careful inspection I've come to the conclusion there are three groups of people who find out:

The ones you need to tell to maintain semblances of your functional side.
The ones who trigger it.
The ones who are digging toward it and are already halfway there themselves -

the latter are rare and perfect.

***

***

You and I.

We are millennials who thought of ourselves as writers who sold out to corporate America and now have to find creative ways to prove we've still retained some kind of personality like wearing a flashy pair of shoes or letting a part of a tattoo show through our dress shirts. I remembered you wanted to be an actor when you were young and I wanted to be a psychologist. Do you think that means something?

I moved to a new apartment, away from the one we used to spend our Saturdays in. I hung the curtains, put down the rugs. You don't know what it looks like here.

I love that I can hear jazz from my window any time of day. It reminds me of your records and how you taught me to put the needle down the first week we met.

***

Do you ever wonder what the people in your favorite house live like?

I used to wish they installed signs on the backs of airplanes big enough that I could read where they were going when I looked at them from the ground. Atlanta. Wichita. Bora fucking Bora.

I think about the guys who no longer love me still jerking off to the thought of me even when I'm long gone. They don't want me there anymore to scream their name because it's easier to visualize me silent the next time they wack off in the shower. Is that unfair? I've been seeking an opportunity to put a copyright on my body so it's unavailable the next time you think of it.

You told me that while we were breaking up,"you didn't have to have sex with someone else to see if you still loved me, why don't you just jerk off like I do?"

Little, biting comments like that initially made me ache for you, want to mold and move mountains for you, covet you (and in a true twist of irony became one of the reasons I knew I could not.)

I always wish I was a master of the smallest things because they mean the most - like braiding my hair or parallel parking (I can't do either.) That's when I first knew I liked you. You stopped to tie your shoe when we were walking and whipped together an extravagant knot and told me to wait up. How many times have we been told you find love in intense, moving ways? You are a testament to the fact the soul-altering is found in common places.

When we got back to the workplace we now shared I texted my friends:
"I think I love the guy I work with. He might be gay."

You can't blame me. You did tie an extravagant knot.

This is how the brain works: it goes all the way from airplanes right back to you.

***

He and I had been having sex for over an hour and I wanted to go home by 12:35. I was committed to this. I was going to fuck somebody else — not *you* — and it was going to be incredible, earth-shattering, awesome.

So, I did.
It happened.
It wasn't.

He jerked off as I sat on the edge of the bed, letting the fan that was helping us through the mid-August sweat cover up the slight sound of my crying.

Crying because it was soulless, soft and awful. Crying because I had snuck in through the backdoor to avoid the party going on in his kitchen two hours ago and neither of us had climaxed. (But, more than likely crying because I'd been off my Lexapro for a week. Not only had you been officially gone for a few days, abruptly stifling my sense of intimacy, but my beloved lightly-medicated brain was edging toward the deep end.)

"Want to try again?" He said.
"No."

I had gotten good — professional even — at this before you; letting physical things happen and pass.

"I'm going to put my shorts on and go."

He was still touching himself when I escaped once again out the backdoor, avoiding his roommates who were now stoned and watching reruns of Springer in the living room. They seemed like generally nice people.

Going 85 down I-75 and I'm noticing my vagina is rubbed raw from his dick because I couldn't get my body to turn on. Be there. Enjoy it. I'm rushing back to the Detroit city line I had chosen so I could run from moments that reared their head at me and no one would follow. Eight Mile. Six Mile. Davison. Warren. Home.

My windows were down and the scent of someone else's Parliaments rolled in — the kind you wouldn't ever let me take a drag of. I thought of you. And the time you held me against the dryer, letting the vibrations of laundry (you had convinced me to do after I hadn't left bed for three days) gently move us closer.

I thought about calling you. I thought about how I used to think all the "treating your body like a temple" hippies were complete frauds even when I was smoking a bunch of weed. I thought about how I may not be ready to treat this vessel like a temple but I needed to find a way to protect it from other bodies who use dryers to move me closer and being rubbed raw time and time again.

***

I passed a rather terrible car accident sitting in the backseat of my aunt's Lexus. She and my mom were driving me to the airport. I'd forgotten to take enough vacation days off for this prolonged family trip. They talked about vegan muffin recipes in the front seats.

It wasn't just a fender-bender. A couple cars were crushed on their sides, paint chipped. In the middle of the median was a man's leather-clad body, his motorcycle a couple inches from his outstretched hand like an overly-American version of the Michelangelo masterpiece.

About a week later I Googled to see if the guy was dead, if his family had been notified, where the service was to be held, if he wanted flowers or donations: click, click, click, it was that easy. His wife's name was Sharon. She seemed wonderful. The obituary said they volunteered together at animal shelters on the weekends.

It was the first dead body I had ever seen
except my own.

I have tried to find better ways to describe it.

"It" being the feeling when you have been on your bathroom floor for an hour and the upper hasn't kicked in yet. The caving in your body does when someone wants to touch you for the first time and you are only 89 percent certain you won't ask them to stay in bed with you for ten days afterward. The moment when you're laying in the sun and thinking of a past love's scent or their teeth or the way you used to cuff their jeans for them makes your extremities feel like you've set up camp in a summit with no plans to descend.

I've asked other people to describe "it" for me too, hoping one response from someone in my life would lead to this genius packaged epiphany I could carry in my back pocket for the sagas where I take three mental health days in a row from work or the next time I am crying in front of a guy who once said he loved me and he asks "why are you like this?"

My friends now tell me to take my pills when I call them asking if they want a pizza delivered at four in the morning on a Tuesday (they're not bad people - that's what I told them to say.)

I don't know how else to say it. I have been so deeply sad and unmoved for years. So, I go with the closest possible thing

I'm dead.

"Let's get champagne."

It was ten in the morning and this was your first real text to me aside from first-message pleasantries (*Hi, what's up, here's my number just in case you need help with anything outside of work, it's really convenient you live right across the street from me, etc.*)

"Is he a contestant on a dating show?" my roommate scoffed after I read the text message aloud for the fourth time over, the simplicity of your statement feeling immense, buzzing in the small device in my palms.

You picked me up in your truck and that's what we did. Six-dollar Andre champagne and two-dollar orange juice from the grocery store around the corner which never had apples but always had whiskey.

Without cups, we swished the concoction around in our mouths ("mouth mimosas") and spit some on the ground of the cab and watched as one of winter's first suns surfaced overhead. As you took us across the MacArthur Bridge to Belle Isle, you told me the massive park was designed by the same man who dreamed up Central Park. You loved this city the way I aspired to.

Later, we sat in the back row of an arthouse movie theater, leaning legs against one another's - the way you do when the intentional first touch is forthcoming and inevitable. You took me to your favorite store, where you knew the owner, to find a Christmas gift for your mother. Still feeling the orange buzz, we picked out a $100 teapot. You took my hand as we hopped your back gate (you'd dropped the keys in your truck and we were moving too fast to try and locate.) You took my face in your hands as we moved closer on your couch - the one missing patches of fabric.

You took me to your bed. You took over. I was taken before 3:00 p.m.

***

***

After you call friends in the thick of the earliest morning hours, breathing into the receiver about how it may be the last time you talk to them, it is hard to surmise what the point of origin was. What makes us spiral? What is the starting point for the need to expire?

I found out later something that should be incredibly apparent from the jump: love should not be that kickstarter. This is why, with our kind of connection, often I am unable to recollect on what made me love you deeply in the first place - aside from that grand knot you tied.

Here are two I have been able to conjure:

1. The perfect o-shape your mouth takes when you fall asleep and despite its spherical silhouette, when I traced its outline with my pointer finger it never felt like I was circling the drain.

2. I would come back to my phone and see a picture of an aluminum camper abandoned in someone's backyard in my messages and you'd ask "is this the one you want?"

***

"I just moved in and don't have a can opener — if you see this in the next hour, SOS."

I emailed that to you before I had your number - flirtation with a hint of desperation in the modern age. I lived in a twelve-story high rise building. Overlooking the avenue separating us I could see the lights go on and off in your windows, something I never told you I looked at, especially when you stopped answering.

"Come over, we're the first door in the duplex, I'll let you in."

I ran over barefoot, irrationally nervous you'd change your mind about my kitchenette rental. James Brown was playing when you threw the door open, pan-in-hand and the smoke alarm sounding in the distance. James was louder.

"Come in, everything's burning."
You smirked.

You handed me the opener I needed for the can back at my place after putting out a small fire. Your zucchini was still edible.

"When'd you move to the city?"
"It's been two weeks. No cable in my apartment still. What about you?"

You eyed me, flipping a slice of zucchini into your mouth.

"Two years, my girlfriend and I moved down here."
"Oh yeah?" I eyed the two bedroom living space.
"She just moved out. I have another roommate moving in next week."
You rambled far past that.

"Why'd you move here?" You asked.
"I love Detroit."
"Detroit's the only city where people will risk practicality for love."
"This was my practical option. It was between this or an island in the Pacific."
"I can picture you on an island."
"Why's that?"
"You showed up on my doorstep barefoot in November."

***

***

I moved to Detroit because it's always felt like it already had been broken in.

It started early

when my grandmother took me to the Penobscot Building when I was six to tapdance in their hallways, to hear the click-clacks echo, bouncing off the golden walls, because there was little foot traffic aside from us. It started when I would sit in trees for hours between the inexplicable jungle vines that attempted to overtake parts of the city, unaware of how many people had forgotten there is beauty here.

The Midwest looks at this city nostalgically. The world views it as ruined. I may have always looked at it as rose-colored but that's how all the greatest (and most tumultuous) loves begin.

There are places in Detroit where churches are the only thing left in a neighborhood.
I don't believe in God but I believe in faith like that.

***

***

I can fuck,
I can bend at the hips,
I can bow at the sun,
I can tell you I'm leaving, I will return the next morning. I can crack my knuckles against your chest, I will ask you to smile as you are inside of me and remember the feeling later, I will drink until I call you and I'll hang up when I hear your sigh and the "what do you need?" I can stop crying when you drop me off on the side of the road, I can count to ten, I can brush your soft curls and hear your "I don't let anyone touch me like this" whispered, but never yelled.

I can fuck you after this stalemate.
I can rip the wispy hair from your shoulders the same way mine is ripped away with my own hands when I think of you now.

I can love you.
I can love you.
I can love you.
I can love you.
I can love you.
I can love you.
I can love you.
I can love you.
I can love you.
I can love you.
I can love you.
I can love you.
I can love you.
I can love you.
I can love you.
I can love you.
I can love you.
I can love you.
I can love you.
I can love you.
I can love you.
I can love you.
I can love you.
I can love you.

I promise it, I know it - I can love you.

***

***

In mid-March, I found you on the porch smoking at 8 a.m., lightning draped across the skyline. You told me the night before you were planning to wake up early to watch the morning storm; I called bullshit. Now, I sat down next to you on the wet wood, your t-shirt almost fitting me — not in an adorable-hanging way — because you were slight then and not much bigger than me.

I leaned my head in for a drag of daybreak smoke and you pulled it away gently but moved your arm around my shoulders as consolation.

"I wasn't expecting this."
"The storm?"
"You."

You were quiet again, puff of smoke.
You were the wettest day of spring,
always smelling like that holy rain —
my personal Pentecost.

Reflecting on it now, as we sat there with navy clouds collecting above us, I took this concise realization as an undercover "I love you." Your permission to bury deeper into your worn t-shirts and the nests I had made in the shallow nooks of your body. Indication that you needed me and I had been let in. Reliance.

As clandestine as ever, you were not accepting this feeling, you were combating it.

Those who feel naturally unlovable should not attach themselves to those unwilling or unprepared to provide love — that's a given — but the knots created and tangled while you're spinning don't become apparent until the noose is a little too tight and you're hanging from it.

I leaned closer as the bolts continued to pass by the Book Tower in the distance. The clouds were moving north, away from us and our little slice of this urban empire. You snuff out your smoke and place your other arm around me, laying your head in my lap. Rain drops collected like dew on the beard you were beginning to grow. They watered you.

I watched you growing.
One of us was there, I was not fighting it.
***

We spent the day side-by-side laying on sand that was closer to mud this time of year because it wasn't considered beach weather in Michigan quite yet.

I wore a white one-piece bathing suit that grabbed the part between my hips and waist that was paler and thicker than I wanted it to be going into the summer months — you tugged at that space adoringly and kissed it and bit it with confidence when I complained.

You kissed that space and pushed harder with every peck and pushed me downward and shoved me further from our blanket into the brown mess beneath us.

The mud was overtaking me and this was the closest I had ever felt to being buried — for a dead girl, this was significant. I was closest to the underground I had ever been. I didn't know it yet, but this progressive interment only happened when I was with you.

Who the hell gets buried wearing white?

I could not yet comprehend the work it would take to dig up the body we were burying together - I loved being this deep.

We went home and showered, picking remains of dried dirt off each other's shoulders the water couldn't purge.

You got out before I did and saw the premature dandelions I picked
sprawled on the kitchen table
and called them "the things she loves."

***

Is the first person you sleep with when you're falling out of love with someone else ever magical? Is it ever soul-pleasing? Is it ever the fulfillment you crave, lost and are seeking?

Is it ever *good*?

I was horizontal most of the time with the first man I tried to replace you with. From sex to sleep, there was little change in position between noon and midnight. We took our meals from his twin-sized bed — hot days made hotter by summertime Campbell's soup. We spent weekends curled in the crevices of his L-shaped couch with static from the television reflected in the beads of sweat on his back.

It is unmistakable how similar activities to those you and I took part in could feel foreign when they're done with someone else.

In the brief moments I was awake, usually while he was pressed tight against me, holding onto the bedpost for dear life, I would look at the sparrows sitting in the birch outside his window. I knew you were out there, continuing, vertically. Riding the bike with the orange handlebars from porches to parties to patios - laughing.

And although I was foregoing calling my mother back, taking my pills, texting my best friend "happy birthday!" — opting instead to take my third nap of the day — it was grossly comforting to me you hadn't slowed down after you left me crying in the driver's seat following that bottle of red we finished before beginning to argue in public. I called it our Last Supper; you called it the last straw.

The little birds from the birch would come to me, whispering that I needed to escape. Instead, I returned to his unfamiliar blankets. I tore the wings off those sparrows whenever they arrived, letting them lay on his window sill, watching me with their last few blinks while he kissed my collarbone.

I never want to leave rooms with gold lighting.

I didn't mind that he kept me inside that summer. I needed to be laying down. The slow walk from his oven to his bed felt exhausting, debilitating.

I was so tired, baby.

***

***

I was trying to learn Spanish when I met you,
but the first time you ran your hands through my hair,
you taught me another language.

After the first months of rapture faded, I learned
"I want to fuck you" doesn't translate to
"I've been thinking about you all day
and I need you to stay here with me."

When I saw you on your birthday,
(the first one celebrated after you left
and the time you pulled me upstairs,
away from the party,
we fought and did coke off your car keys)
I learned we'll always speak in you-remember-this-about-me's and
I-remember-when-you-said-that's.

We still talk in the hushed language of "we used to love each other."

***

***

The most vulnerable position someone can be in is sitting at the edge of their bed,
back toward you while the lights are still out.

You did that a lot, back toward me.

Suddenly you would turn and tell me it made sense my twenty-third birthday fell in late August
because I reminded you of a sundown after a hot day.

Then you would put on your leather belt I had taken off the night before and we'd get in your
truck and drive to work but my brain would hum all day with the feeling of possessing your
entirety before 6:00 a.m.

I never asked for details on why the end of August and I were made for each other.
I knew it was true.

***

***

Men are funniest when they want to fuck you.

Not funny in the way that will make you laugh, but rather, hysterical because they reveal the part of their brain I am never going to (and not willing to) comprehend.

"*Your mouth is fuckable.*" - Guy at dive bar.
I ended up face down on his bathroom floor while his roommates played video games in the living room.

"*My wife isn't living in the house anymore.*" - Forty-something man who works three cubicles over from me.
Follows me to the parking lot at five.

You didn't say anything before we touched for the first time and this is how I'll always imagine you; crawling toward me, quietly. It was a comfort on the nights I knew you were six whiskeys deep, draped over a bar without me. Or the days you would spend with your friends - the few I wasn't allowed to meet because I knew you weren't ever able to sit in comfortable silence with them.

In the days you started to turn away, picturing you coming closer gave me confirmation I hadn't made you up. I'll admit, I did place imaginary, metaphorical significance on these silent moments in the immediate months after your departure.

Like what it meant that sometimes you'd stop mid-sentence when our eyes locked. The similes and metaphors I derived from the image of your body encapsulated in the dark, the record ending behind you and the full-stop your body did when you let yourself lean into me.

When you let yourself collapse across my chest.

When you let me trace hearts onto your scalp with the tender tips of my thumbs.

When you let me love you. When you opened.

***

***

I found you in a deep-seated crevice,
I found you rolled tight,
I found you aching, I found you fetal.

Months later, I woke up and discovered the ivy tops of half-eaten strawberries scattered across
your bed after a night of gin and not much else.
The leftover crimson juices stained your gray sheets deeply
because when you moved
and when I moved
we painted with them.

"Turn it off" you breathed, already sitting straight toward me as the morning alarm chimed. There
was enough time to make it back to my apartment to rinse, only so you can pick me up again.
There was not enough time under these covers.

I silenced it, I rolled back over, you rolled back in.

***

***

"Are you sure he wasn't just using you for sex?" - Someone who thought that was a good thing to say to me.

Relationships that are strictly about sex need to be as consensual as the sex itself.
I never said yes to that.

***

***

Have you ever heard a song while you were driving and thought, "if I ran off the road while listening to this, I would be okay with that ending?"

Have you ever rolled down all the windows in subzero temperatures to see if the wind catches your hair the same way it can in July?

It does.

I had a professor in college who told us research indicates you will have the most important conversations of your life in kitchens and cars. He said now that we knew this, we'd think about that statistic any time it happened to us.

That is why we spent an hour laughing and lying on your kitchen floor, my head curved into the sacred space between your lungs and ears, forgetting about the brussels sprouts in the oven.

That is why I told you I loved you while I straddled you in the driver's seat, my brain buried deep inside the headrest.

***

***

I bought a six hundred dollar plane ticket to New York on New Year's Eve to escape the notion my brain had created that there was a .03 percent chance you were going to call me and request to spend it together.

I drank two bottles of champagne on a rooftop in Brooklyn. I kissed my gay best friend that night while the fireworks crashed across the city from panoramic angles. On December 31st, I had the best sex of my life in Bed-Stuy with a guy I met while dancing to Tupac in a bar that had quotes written in neon on the walls. Incredibly millennial. You would've hated it.

Between takes he asked me why I loved Detroit and why I didn't live in Brooklyn instead and I talked so much, when I messaged him later thanking him for the night he said his opinion on the city he'd never visited had changed.

No metaphor here - I thought you may be proud of me.

***

***

A visitor once told me she knew Detroit was a woman.

But, they told us no love was left in this city,
and we found it -
we discovered ways to breathe life into our own.

And, we found there is adoration
in the eyes of everyone here.

And, we found she sits but she doesn't wait -
she is untamed.

She is unrivaled -
and she is this city and
this is home.

***

***

We found him and we named him after a main artery of our city, Beaubien - Beau for short.

He was a shrimpy pup with a limp, a brown spot that encased a cataract left eye and a bark which squeaked uncharacteristically high for a dog who looked like he'd previously been a fighter.

He was running down the service drive next to 94, attempting to climb through a hole in the fence nearing the freeway. You threw your bike in the grass, running toward him, crouched and hand out. He approached immediately, entwining himself at your ankles and going belly-up for a stroke. You carried him, with the fleas we didn't know about yet and all, back to the crate on your bike and we carried on. Your red high-tops made us look like Leave it to Beaver characters, two kids and a pup in our basket, cruising through gardens and across old train tracks toward our sunny front porch.

You can't do that in most cities anymore — find a tagless dog wandering through traffic, pop it into the back of the bike and take it to a home where you're sure a friend who walks through your door will take it and adore it. You can't do that anywhere anymore - that takes a community that will lean and love and learn.

Our city depends on being a home to the kind of people who won't let neighborhood dogs get stuck in fences. Houses next to each other seem to lean on their more sturdy neighbors, and that's how Detroit's people are too - taking part in the oldest practice of humankind, taking care of their own. Prideful in those who choose to stick it out and letting others lean when they need an anchor or a hand or a port in the storm.

We petted and stroked and played with Beau from noon until evening and then Beau hopped into the truck bed of a friend of yours who needed a guard dog. I didn't think he'd be especially good at that job with his limp, but he received love for an entire day and that seemed like the best kind of day to him.

***

You were in metamorphosis when we met.

Unsure of the clothes you wore and the people you were beginning to associate with, you asked for my guidance. I wonder if you still ask whoever's lying next to you for validation or whether you're comfortable enough now to look in the mirror and decidedly wear the green shirt today.

Here's the thing I won't hide — I was insecure too — my uncertainties made you say, "why can't you believe I want to be with you without me saying I love you?"

This is what I know to be true about those who are still piecing themselves together; they steal important parts from people who have spent years molding themselves on their own. For instance, I was always afraid of driving over bridges — I never meant it to become my quirk — something friends would reference whenever we took on infrastructure,

"Shut your eyes, we're going over a bridge."

You took several habits from me, I took a couple of your socks you left under my bed. I know I'm not strictly a victim but you set fire to my mind and now and again you returned to burn the bridge.

***

"I can't tell you I love you," you said.
"Because you don't?"
"Because I don't know what this is."
"So, it could be love?"
"It isn't."
"Are you sure?"
"I want you here."

It's simple; offering love to a chosen human is the most significant thing our primate hands can grasp. To see you deny this sacred sentence, to me, was a mania-inducing quandary: If someone who had so assuredly ripped through layers to find a heart I didn't know I had resting there couldn't say they loved me, who was going to see me dripping in magic-hour-honey light, nakedly dancing to bluegrass in the living room and frantic at a bartender's last call, who was going to see me there and there and over there and tell me they loved me if you could not do me that favor? You fed me these dry substitutes as solace.

For god's sake, could you have told me you loved me to calm me?

(Rationally, I never would have asked you to do that. Although, I often wonder why you dug yourself all the way to this core if you weren't going to do anything with the molten you came across.)

I lingered, seeking this age-old answer in an effort to avoid having to find another body who encountered me the same way. I had decided the search was over.

My detached head had made up its mind, there was nothing left over there for me.

***

***

"Let me know when you finally move to that island and I'll come with."

A midday message I received from a number that was not familiar anymore after three months of silence.

Maybe you were fed up with the unintended corporate path you'd chosen when you switched jobs/maybe you had been daydreaming.

"The island's waiting, still in my plans — I'm ready when you are."

I responded, but not with that. Sometimes I indulge in thinking about what could be altered if we all said what we meant in the heat of it.

***

"Okay."

I just told you about the days my brain deactivates and — on the other side of my spectrum — the times it awakens, arteries revving wild enough to call you twelve times in the middle of the night to ask whether you think we will last into the summer.

It was a particularly warm day in April, the windows in your house were open for the first time. The strongest sun we had seen in months; it created simple shadows that reverberated against the kitchen tile. You had gotten back from a two-week trip across the ocean. The bracelet you intended to bring back to me had gotten confiscated at Customs.

An hour earlier, your neighbors had caught us kissing while we laid on the picnic table in your backyard. We talked ourselves off its chipped ledge and went inside.

I hadn't wanted to die then — that's why I told you. At a moment where I felt open enough to share the secret I had only ever sobbed into the backsides of pillows or shouted from the back of my internal horse on the frontlines I manned, defending myself from that cranial enemy who impedes my existence, or during the mornings I woke up and clawed at my hair while thinking about how I either let people set me alight like Roman candles or I let them go entirely.

"Okay," you said again.

"I'm going to hold you here for a minute," you said.

We sat on the patched couch where we had kissed for the first time.
I loved your skin that was touching me and the being it protected and the scar serving as an equator between the two sides of your chest.
I pounded on the left side -
that thing wasn't hollow.
I knew then I was never going to give away that love,
the only way it would fade is if you left first.
Even then, I wasn't sure it would dissolve.

"I don't know what to say right now."
"There's nothing to say."

You continued speaking as if I hadn't whispered my comment into the crook of your shoulder. Maybe you hadn't heard me.

"But I think I will soon."

***

You let me rub your already suntanned temples as we flew kites on our Detroit island. Your magnificent dragon floated lightly with the breeze. Your head on my lap, we watched freighters sail through the strait and drank red wine from empty water bottles we had recovered from your recycling bin. You braided the darker strands on the inside of my hair - something your mother taught you to do - and turned me around when you finished. The early May sunlight hit my eyes, and as my pupils adjusted you took a good look at me.

"Those eyes aren't fair," you said.

You remembered my license listed my eyes as "gray" - my "interesting" icebreaker from one of our first dinner table talks, but you were convinced they took on more of a laurel green hue on sunny afternoons.

At the close of our day, the end of your torso tasted like dried sweat and sweeter than powdered sugar while your gums tasted like the last cigarette I watched you throw out the car window on the way back to your house.

Every moment of you I have kept enshrined is distinctly black and white in my memory now and as tame as Big Sky horses, as you always were.

***

So this is it,
the part where the angels come and take our good stuff at night.

And leave only the parts we have to sort out in the morning.
They leave us to wonder where we stowed the valuables
we had found in each other,
we looked in the attic and we searched between the annuals.
We checked the notes we had written,
thanking the gods we never went to worship
that we had found another person
who could bare our weight
and match the raw levels of affection we exude.

We checked to make sure the signatures we had put there were valid
and in the black ink
important things like this
require.

For a time, we both thought we had really found something here.

We cried out for the cream of it to return,
along with the heart we thought we had earned.

We blamed this betrayal on the heavenly so we didn't have to figure out
who started our slide.

So this is it,
that is where we launched and this is where we landed.

***

***

We went to a concert at a dive bar a few miles from your place. Seven people showed up excluding me and you.

You danced like Freddie Mercury while I drank a Stroh's — I knew you wanted me to join but I was inadvisably angry you had used GPS directions to get here, taking us onto the freeway, rather than going the scenic route.

When the show wrapped and I had put back a few more, you lit up a cigarette on the ride home. Marlboro Reds. Not yours, you must have taken them from someone else. Maybe from your neighbor - the man who bought the abandoned house next to yours, where he spends his days stripping wood and building staircases.

You offered me a drag. I put my mouth on it, deep purple lipstick staining the white.

It was the first time you let me smoke with you.

We had sex on the living room floor that night. When you came, you left me lying on the mustard-colored carpet waiting for you to come back with a rag or a beach towel or your hands.

"Get up." I heard you say from the open door to your bedroom. I came to your mattress the same way I had followed you there after our first day together and you still tucked me in and kissed my head and touched my shoulder when I rolled away. But, my eyes shot open four times that night, the taste of cloves and tar waking me.

When it was all over I went back and checked the invite details from that concert. "10 p.m., BYOB - the bartenders don't care. April 25th."

I knew the exact date you started to go.

***

***

In the six months after we broke up:
1. I cut six inches of my hair off
2. Dyed it black
3. Got a tattoo that looks like it also could've been procured from a jailhouse pen

If I was fifteen and had also wanted a tongue piercing, it would have all been considered "going through something" but they were genuine, retroactive steps taken toward unattractiveness.

I thought if I couldn't have you lean over and breath the bassline of the song on the radio into my ear as I sat in your passenger seat with my feet rested on the glovebox I did not want to have that long blonde hair or clean skin. I did not need to attract anyone else because hearing you say "you're most beautiful when you're naked" had felt like it filled me and I needed nothing else.

***

***

The thought of your scent is still my biggest pitfall.
It is smoke and mint and dollar shampoo.

Remembering your phrases throws me back into it too:
"You look your best when you smile like that."
Or, "isn't the way the light hits that window really, really, really gorgeous?"

Or thinking of the lapsing moments you would remember I was a little bit younger, a little more ready, a little less wild. But young, ready and wild all the same. I think somewhere along the way you also realized I was not as graceful as the Sunday morning coffee we drank or as mature as the Wednesday night touches in your living room.

I had to start apologizing for the way my worst habits always derive from my best intentions.

When these all factored together, we laid in your bed, taking turns flipping the pages until the corners got soggy from our combined spit. You had to tell me when the book ended and how it finished and where we ended up

because I had drown out the possibility of leaving months before.

***

***

It was in the quietest hours that you came across strongest.
Your beard prickling nerves deep underneath my skin, my hands bent backwards so hard against your chest that these thin blue rivers became visible.

I had never had a valentine before.

We woke up on the 14th and had sex in my bathtub the water red from my period. When I was on top I kept thinking about how my seventh grade science teacher said you could drown in one inch of liquid if you tried hard enough. There wasn't any water left in the tub when we were done.

We drove to a drive-in movie theater in the evening. No blankets or thick coats, but we sat through a Michigan winter double-feature in your truck bed anyway. You wanted to take a drive after — we slid down suburban streets, sailing into the cul-de-sac of your childhood home, the one your parents had fought in. You would only tell me once or twice about hiding in your bedroom during their battles. You leaned over the console and whispered something I hadn't heard before.

"I don't know what happened here."

We staked out the home you used to inhabit for twenty minutes, as the older couple who moved in after sat closely on their floral couch watching late-night television in their bathrobes. Conan or Kimmel, I think.

We pulled away without a farewell. As we drove the six miles home I saw the console expand between us. You dropped me off at my apartment and told me you didn't want to share your bed tonight. You had seen my panic and my sadness in the daytime and stayed, the light so strong it was able to glare back at you. I hadn't thought you would start leaving at night.

You had given me an inch and I had drown in it.

***

***

Friends at the bar the other night discussed how the seriousness of their relationships came later than the first encounter. How Hollywood has given us this fictitious idea that we will know someone's the end-all-be-all within those first few moments.

They thought everyone around the table was in consensus. *Of course* we all understood the absurdity of that. They didn't even ask me to concur before moving to a new topic — I never talked about love in a friendly way.

I swirled my gin quietly instead of telling them it happened to me and I think about it often.

That's one thing you couldn't remove from me. I would let the entirety of the human race trace fingers all the way to whatever part of our celestial limbic system controls memory if it let them experience that instance of breathlessness I had when I saw you. The one I did not believe in either (the one I haven't been able to recreate since then.) I have tried to erase a majority of the memories I initially carried away with me but I will forever retain the fire-to-the-gut, blood-pressure-spiking, impale to the heart I felt when you looked back at me in that first moment.

***

***

You made me feel like the beauty marks on both corners of my mouth — the permanent markers I was always conscious of — had been speckles making up Orion himself, not just his belt, left behind by whoever paints our silhouettes and places us in these bodies.

***

***

The last day we were distinctly together didn't give me a sign that it was the last of anything.

I had shown up on your patio two hours ago, wearing a new sundress even though the weather was still turning.

"Does this not fit me right?"
"I want to hide you."

So, we hid.

For a couple hours that faded into evening, we covered all our normal spaces in record time - the floor of the bathroom, the edge of your bed, against the sliding door in the living room, the couch in the corner. Rubbing up and down your forearms and your bare chest and the dimples of your spine and your hands doing the same - no kisses, just placed faith in our memorized movements. I bent backward to hear you breathe. We were uncovered.

I led and you followed - our touches acting in parabola. Our silent lexicon. My mind wasn't hushed though — even with your hands gripping my most vulnerable parts, I wandered. I thought about how you chose to hide me from your friends, and from your mother when she came to visit. But, the way you didn't ever hide our bodies from wide open windows mystifies me now that I'm gone.

I love the way our human touch is a form of human error.

When we finally arose there was a half hour left to get to the ice cream stand three blocks from us. We made it in time, poked each other's gums with our tongues that were stained blue from flavored slush. It was dark on our bike ride back and I kissed you at the front gate, in front of the lawn flamingo. We said our goodbyes and you tugged at my hair, extending your arm as you walked to your door, letting my hair catch a breeze as you released it.

I never did make it back into our familiar little domain after that. You moved to another part of the city before I could. When I drive by that oasis we spent the winter in now, the exterior is olive — it doesn't shine quite like it did when sunsets beamed off the old white paneling.

I am convinced this is why you left,
I took you away from sunlight too often.

***

***

I am the product of being told my breasts were "too big for my body" by a male coach when I was twelve, who felt if my physique could somehow shift overnight I would see success. I am what comes after your mother hears from a friend's father that your number of sexual partners hit double digits (because he was *just* trying to "protect me.")

I am the result of laying naked next to the boy I had just lost my virginity to and being told "this is the last time this will happen."

What am I supposed to think?

Everything has a balancing point
everyone has a tipping point.

What's yours, what's yours, what's fucking yours?

***

At dawn today, I realized there are three
months til' my twenty-fifth.
She's finally here and she's heaven
and she's having to figure out what this quarter has meant.

I sent my first nude photo when I was fourteen.
When I was fourteen,
when I was fourteen,
when I was fourteen,
when I was fourteen.

What was there to show?
Besides the lines just beginning to change
at the corners of my hips.
And the face of certainty
that *this* was the way to further how I felt.

What was there to show?
Other than what my mother wasn't allowed to see anymore.
Other than the stained mirror and the shower curtain I had not picked, draped behind me.
An illusion- my body was not yet curtailed to fit the curve of the sink.
That curve, my first canyons,
forming - when I was fourteen.

She is older and she is still here and she is heaven -
I want you to know this is the best I'll ever have it.

***

"Just let me hold on to you."

But I can't let you do that right now — the thought of anyone annexing me is too heavy and my arms flare with smoke and then heat and then fever while you try to bring me close. I'm pacing back and forth in front of your bed while you lay stoically after letting your arms drop back to your sides. Eventually I'll say "I cannot be near you right now" and I'll grab a sweatshirt from one of your open drawers and I will be back in my bed just across the street in less than seven minutes and I will think about the ways in which your touch may have affected me but never about how you looked when I abandoned what we had deemed comfortable.

If I wouldn't let you hold me when you were the most cherished, then why was I tied to you, and then your shadow, for months? It was your straight-lined upper teeth and the bottom's disarray, I could not make promises to someone so ideal. The glimmer of your skin on unexpected warm days underneath the jean shorts you cut too short by yourself with kitchen scissors.

What came first, the men who did not handle me like china packed in a box labeled "fragile" or this uncontrollable feeling of resentment?

No one is designed this way. I encountered this somewhere and absorbed.

***

***

I am pinned against the side of the house, I'm sixteen — he hasn't told me he loves me yet but he said he will after he slips it in. His hand is on my neck and the other is pulling down the sweatpants I got from playing on the junior varsity volleyball team. I had begged my mother to pay the extra few dollars to have my last name embroidered inside the waistband. Inside the home I was pressed against I had been getting ready to sleep in a bunk bed with a girlfriend — he had pulled me away from there.

Everyone else at the party had passed out in armchairs and on tile floors which were colder than the rest of the house on a June night. I could see them through the floor-to-ceiling windows I was facing — his stocky shoulders came right up to my nose.

"You're too tight."

He fidgeted for a moment longer before he decided he would see me inside instead, kissing me on the cheek before I heard the screen door slam. I stayed outside a minute longer, sitting still while my brain zigged and zagged toward the resolution that we were now somehow connected in an exclusive way.

Even now, I don't count this as "losing it." I lost something closer to an all-consuming innocence that night, but it was not losing a virginity I obsessed about giving away. He did eventually take it from me though: I snuck into his house five months later with snow inbetween my toes. I could settle for this bargain — I knew he was the only boy that wanted me.

I knew then interactions like this wouldn't help me identify love.
I thought I would get better.

***

***

I was able to think of a few additional moments in which I knew I loved you, after that first knot you tied around me:

1. Whispering dirty-nothings in your ear under the yellow blanket your grandmother knit for you back in the "old country."
2. Leaning over as you're driving to rest my head uncomfortably on your shoulder and biting the hanging parts of your beard hard enough that you laugh and knock the windshield wipers on.
3. Stomping on the frostbitten, rising perennials while sneaking in your window because it was a more direct route to you than the front door.
4. Knowing during the innumerable days that make up Michigan winters, you were waiting for me in the warmest place.

***

You thought my hands only wrapped around your waist when you would leave me in bed and I couldn't get up to go to work. You thought they only grabbed the steering wheel when you'd forget you were driving as you regaled me with a story. You thought they only genuinely felt you when I would wake up from rough sleep, needing you in me to cure the mania I had dreamed up - always that you were going to leave before every sunrise.

Did you memorize my palms the same way I etched the slope of your nose into the backs of my eyelids with my fingernails? Carved so deeply into my memory, I see your profile like residual flash from a camera whenever the lights turn off and I flutter to sleep.

Comparing people to addictions is trite. I won't compare you to the substance, the experience of you is the true zenith. All highs feel distinctly new but they're all unsustainable. Like a bona fide junkie, I couldn't keep my hands wrapped around the feeling forever
something had to give.

I was constantly worried.
Was I going to lose you to the sun that leaks through the crack in your window?
Was I going to slip up and let my fingers fall away at the first sign of you taking flight in spring?

I would rather give you up altogether than watch you leave in pieces.

***

"You only loved me because I was the first person who cared about you here."

You were still holding the palm-sized plant I had bought for your housewarming. I've wondered if you threw it out after I fled your new porch or whether it still soaks up sun on a windowsill close to you.

"That's not why." I cracked hard here.
"I don't know what you made this into."

When the person who has been on the receiving end of every gift you have ever offered another individual throws everything but the kitchen sink it's hard to understand how they can so coolly slide back to the outside and begin tapping on your glass without apology.

"I think you know what we are and what we have been," I said.

Your gaze shifted from me to the oak tree in your front lawn. A neighborhood cat jumped onto the porch to watch us dig the final nails into this.

"I never understood you," you said. "And now it feels like you're begging."

You had already started talking to someone new. I knew.
You had to discount me to move seamlessly into something new. I did not know that was a possibility.

I ran down your front stairs and got my hair caught in the car door as I closed it.
You did not watch me drive away.
You did not call out to apologize.

Even as I ran every red light home and pulled to the side of the road to pronounce myself dead once again through blurred vision, I envied you. I envied your conviction and your ability to distinctly know when you were through — I have tried to model you in many ways, but I have never learned to do that.

***

***

I hadn't bled the first time around so I bled all over his forest green sheets for good measure - school colors, how quaint.

My body wanted to impress that first boy so rabidly that it had waited until I didn't care the second time around to let go. I did care, I just wasn't conscious. Conscious is not the right word cognizant feels better.

I was not cognizant.

It started in the bathroom of another dorm room, and once the objectively cuter boy had pulled my roommate in the other direction, I was dragged another way into a room down the hall and he appraised me. He looked me up and down, scanning for blatant errors, and then touched and I fell backwards into the forest sheets as he pulled down a skirt I had bought on sale earlier that day.

I went to see a school-sponsored therapist the next week at the student health center and she said I shouldn't think too much about it because then I will "make it into something it wasn't."

My problem was I didn't think I was thinking about it enough, considering what it was, and after I was told to keep my mouth shut and my thoughts low like I had been told to keep my legs shut, I did not think about it again.

I did not think about how his touch mattered. I didn't think about my blood dripping down the side of the fake siding on the bed — I bled so much. It stained my underwear, somehow the armpits of my shirt. I found swatches of dried clots in my hair the next day.

I did not think my distrust for men's hands could grow deeper and more cavernous. I did not think my self-imposed unwillingness to allow new touches could get as thick as a forest and continue budding until it was something I couldn't evade.

***

My mania was extraordinary to me.

A no-strings-attached bounceback from the grease-stained dishes that surrounded my bed like an approaching army. It was an opportunity to buy six grand pianos I would never learn to play (but I knew they would look pretty lined up side-by-side in a living room) and a time to glue the pieces of my bed back together that had shattered when I let earthquakes roll through here without ever waking from deep, glorious depression sleep.

I could talk again — I could stay out until 2 a.m. with surface-level friends and laugh about trivial mentions of old flames and shower when it felt right. I could look at pictures of you.

The most thrilling part? I never knew how long these highs would last so I would decide to go to the bar at 11:30 a.m. and put every palm down my pants because I didn't know if I would feel heat that intensely again. And I didn't make plans for dying from up there. Honestly, I didn't have the courage to hop from a high like that — after all, I had to wait for the grand pianos to arrive and stick around for the spontaneous trip to Halifax in May I had booked.

The day before a fall, I could feel it. And I would get my kicks in like stopping the doom clock hinged on how much gin and cocaine I could put in my system under the wire. But, it always struck and I always tipped. And I would decide in those last few minutes before falling flat that, in fact, I *was* going to learn how to play Flight of the Bumblebee.

The armies always returned and I was gone again.

***

It's stunning that a city that was told to "go at it" on its own can cradle you; the feeling you get when your mother's hand rests on your shoulder. It's because it knows what it feels like to be left behind, to be told to "stand up on your own." To once know the glory of love and then to be shunned by people who flee at the first sign of structure and normalcy degrading, breaking.

This is how Detroit raises you - it gives you the reigns and says "finish what came before you."

There is no blank slate, it's the process of picking up where others left off — Grand Boulevard is still lined with the remnants of grandiose the road claims its name from. Flowers across the city still bloom in perennial despite what the house on the lot next to them looks like. For a city that people assume is stagnant, it's the most arduous and most delicate test of personal progress.

When you're someone's protector and they leave without warning it's a punch to the gut. You have failed. I couldn't let the city that leaves me in awe feel like it had let me down — I knew this when I spent days alone exploring corners of its 138 square mile spread. I know this now when I find myself shaking.

Detroit will lean into your anger *and* your love if you let her.

When I needed it most Detroit protected my heart tenfold - the most beautiful portrayal of what can rise from heartbreak. I cannot compare myself to a place that was once called the Paris of the Midwest, the country's manufacturing soul. Its downfall - artistry in its ashes. She's much more exquisite than my own falling outs.

Detroit did not fail me when I was caving.
I can't ever leave.

Build me a house on Flower Street. I can't use a hammer well but I'll help bring the light in.

We can nail roses in haphazard zig-zags to the wooden siding. We can finger paint — or scratch with charcoal — each other's dimples onto the boards of the attic so no one can see them but us. People will come to visit us though. They don't plow this little court in the seemingly infinite winter days, but we will make the way.

We are the only house on the block, and when it's summer we will invite others to pitch tents in our field because I want people in and out always. I want coffee on the stove that disappears because so many hands touch it. We hang our laundry from that dollar store technicolor string we tie from tree to tree, they flap with every gust of wind, they are the petals of our Flower Street. We lay under our oak trees without a sense of what hour is striking and let the leaves pile on us, bodies becoming encased by one another's arms under the autumn residue.

How extraordinary it is that we will still lay next to people who are our phantom limb aches because they temporarily provided us a home. I wanted to share this imaginary home with you and I choose to trust in my delicate daydream rather than our actual ending.

That is the marvelous, steady life I still want that has become the dream it was always meant to be.

That is our life on Flower Street.

***

***

The last time I kissed you I wish I could have made poppies grow from my fingertips like a cheap birthday magician, or make you float above your mattress for a moment, or bite your lips hard enough that you bled back into me.

Anything for a moment where you'd look at me with any kind of intent once again.

***

Today, I could put a finger through my heart and plug the holes in it — the ones I have always been certain are there — while my brain detaches from its stem and settles on the floor for everyone to see. We can all stop what we are doing and observe how that thing operates - maybe I will learn a thing or two.

Confirming with friends the woman you have been seeing has a body straight from the textbook of "*If You Want to Get Fucked.*"

Knowing the skin connecting my vagina and upper thigh is thin and is the largest hem flaw I have making it easier for everything to rip open if I get on my knees and succumb to the serotonin that has never fired on all cylinders.

Puking on a piece of paper, hanging it on my brick wall and calling it "art that came from the inside."

I tried taking myself off my medication today.
This mindset is temporary for me because I am privileged
but it is a grinding, halting, haunting kind of permanent
for those who have no entitlements,
and in turn,
no control.

***

***

The pills are making me fat.

You wouldn't have pried at these "cute" layers of skin. I scratch the parts of my legs that I am positive are expanding by inches every moment I continue to live. I've scratched red irritation patches in neat squares that line up like planets in a decent formation down my thigh - not my best work.

Is this worth it? I do not think controlling my impulses is worth making amends with who I've tried to construct and telling her she's not welcome here.

***

***

Some days when I want to die I picture myself in a floor length silk robe, standing in a backyard in Southwest Detroit with really green grass. And I have collected wind chimes from every coast and I've hung them so they clatter consistently, even during the winter. I have box-dyed red hair and I smoke Marlboros and I can look over my broken white picket fence and see the 1972 Chevy truck I bought from someone else's front yard.

At first, I'm never sure if it's you in the kitchen behind me, yelling my name, but someone's there, slicing avocados or pulling apart tangerines. The knife against the cutting board echoes and I can feel I'm not alone.

Someone joins me in this really green grass as the breeze passes through the chimes and, my god it's loud. It is so loud that I can't hear the person next to me as they say, "I don't want you to blow away."

They laugh in a low hum and when they exhale I can tell it is your breath and I turn and I grab a tangerine slice from your hand and I laugh and laugh and laugh along with.
Maybe you come back. Maybe the grass will get *that* green one of these springs. Maybe I'll throw that stupid fucking robe in the oven. For just a minute, I am blooming.

***

***

Red skies at night will be a sailor's eternal delight. Who knew they would be my reminder that you splintered whenever I asked you how you got here — to our city, where you came from, who you loved — when those cardinal colors panned out before us during sunsets on Belle Isle. It wasn't our Pacific island runaway dream, but it sufficed.

I didn't see before you pushed away that I spit shards of glass on the table in front of you and,
that same color of sundown crimson dripping from my mouth,
made you try to explain to me
why I was hurting.

You couldn't, I couldn't.

How inconceivable it is to have a brain that allows neither intimacy nor complete rejection of these human chemicals — it floats right there in that sweet spot, making you kneel and beg the person in front of you to explain what you have become.

***

***

I arrived on the island around noon and quickly I spilled into the sand, letting the willow trees sway and leave their parts across my chest for the remainder of the day.

An older gentleman woke me by tapping me on the shoulder. He told me I shouldn't be out here alone as the sun was coming down.

But I knew my city caressed us and would not hurt me in any way I couldn't handle or wrap my head around. Hands may touch me but she had already wrapped me up within herself. I looked at him straight and asked if he had fallen in love here and as he backed away from me quickly he said "no." At least he answered.

I didn't know whether I was asking if he had loved here on this island or this city or in this life but I had done all three at once and it often made me fall asleep under willows, the island calling me to spend eternity in the place where love had finally chosen me.

I couldn't resist.

***

***

"Well, you don't ever fix this, you just neutralize it," the doctor said.

I had felt so good and fresh and revitalized and triumphant on my new pills, I had promptly decided to take myself off of them for several weeks. I had finally found nirvana, who needed synthetics? When I once again began to fixate on ways to jump out of windows during meetings and get in low-impact car accidents every time I was behind the wheel, I thought I should seek professional advice.

"I thought I was cured," I admitted to her meekly and childishly, in the comforting environment of sterile tools and fake flowers on the counter next to plastic gloves.
"This is a forever condition it never disappears."
"So, I'm stuck like this?"
"For all intents and purposes, if that's how you want to look at it, yes."

I was not upset about officially being cemented into a brain I already knew I possessed — I had broken my own heart by briefly convincing myself that I had healed it all on my own.

***

***

I have taken a lot of pills — the downers I was prescribed a couple weeks ago — I am laying on my bathroom floor. The crown molding is cut rough and doesn't quite meet the other corner correctly. My apartment building was built as a hotel in the 1940s, the craftsmanship is intricate and done with love and I'm assuming this woodwork isn't the original. The bathtub is running behind me, I pulled out chunks of my hair and they float at the top with the leftover pubic hair I had shaved off the last time I knew I would be having sex.

For being dead for so long, this low feels new and refreshing to me.

I left the light on next to my bed, my dirty dishes rot in the sink just a room away. I have never swept in here, there are balls of my blonde hair wrapped up in the corners by the door too — you told me once I would shed myself away.

I had never noticed my bathroom ceiling was made of weathered white marble, but I'm laying here on the bathroom rug I bought for my first apartment and this vantage point feels significant.

The bulb has burned out by my bed, that crown molding is touching now. I wake up, it's 4 a.m. The overflow bath water creates a small lagoon around me.

It is a year later and I have gone to Europe for the second time. I cried standing in front of the original *Sunflowers*. I looked up and saw the green beams of the Northern Lights played like piano keys, after waiting outside until I became frigid. I thought about how this will all seem hazy in just a few moments too, but I almost died under marble ceilings thinking I wasn't capable of seeing anything this beautiful anymore.

***

Like Van Gogh, I replaced my ears.
I glued flowerbeds on top of the bottomless caverns that were left,
so everything you whispered to me sounded rose-colored.
This way, I could get past the wondering and analysis
of why you could sell me silence as an alternative to sentimentality.
When you had no reason to block me out,
I remembered we didn't ever abandon logic,
we had never possessed it
in the first place.

One evening in late May we got high on your roommate's leftover weed we had found in the medicine cabinet and you told me I had hair like wheat fields and a mouth like a lion's. I sucked on your shoulder, using my canines to leave shallow impressions.

"It opens really wide."
"Does it?" I said.
"And your hair's not like a field it's like a lion too."
"Yeah?"
"And you know me really well."

The most complete compliment you'd given me since our inception.

"Why does the lion like me?"
"She loves you."

***

***

You came with sticks
and you felt my bones.
You came with hands,
you touched
the parts that flutter under pressure.
You came with baby blues
That melt into a shade of purple
When you take acid
And you're laughing.
You came with a mouth

That found my center
every time.

You came with a grasp
that kept me barricaded in your picture window
you had filled with dried bouquets
far longer than I should have
stayed.

***

***

The magic of the golden hour was my clearest path from your hungry hands to your uninhibited heart - something about the dimming, slowing, sinking light filled you with the need to be covered, touched and glowing.

My illumination studies.

You were only truly mine for a minute, or just for that hour when we watched the sun melt into deep blues from the hole-ridden roof of your neighbor's house. You may have belonged to me for our whole several month run — I'll never tell.

Before me, did you know what it's like to tear the wings of someone you love?

On that August eve,
you breathed, you breathed.

***

***

I used to plan for what I would do when you came back.

As you grew further I began to wonder "what will I do when one of us leaves the city we love?" What is my feeling when there are hundreds of miles between us? What is my reaction when I'm eating breakfast with another man and I realize it has been three years and I won't ever play the willing martyr to your empty, purple gaze again? I am certain I will want to know what those eyes have seen once you hit 100 years old. It will be grand, it will be vast — I am preemptively proud of you.

"You're so passive, sometimes I would fuck you just to see if you were feeling something."

I found out during one of our last fights my most intimate, opening moments were your barometer. This is where I had my first real choice - how should I use the unfamiliar space you had created within my chest cavity?

I chose this:
When your heart breaks, you let it break wide open.
I promised I would never touch myself while thinking of the men who left me bare.
But, I'm still going to touch myself.

***

"Thank you. I love you, I'll be there soon."

I was sitting next to an older woman in her sixties or seventies, her neck scarf tied in a neat knot, her pleated skirt ironed professionally, but probably something she learned years ago, while waiting for a flight to New York. It was the third ticket I'd bought in the last two months to escape the city I claimed to love for a larger and far more ferocious urban setting. I was picking anonymity over responsibility.

She was talking on the phone when she spoke these words with quiet, succinct purpose to whoever was fortunate enough to be on the receiving end. The most beautiful sentences I'd ever heard encompassing everything a human can possibly want to hear from another in brevity. The Hawaiian call a similar string of words "Ho'oponopono" - these words placed next to one another are total forgiveness.

I knew you slowed down a little bit to wait for me in the months we were together, and I didn't get the opportunity to catch up. I always wanted to tell you that if I got my medicine mixed right or when the sun came out permanently I'd be able to keep up. To catch up. To be with you. "I'll be there soon."

I used to ask for your patience, now all I will ask for is your kindness.

You couldn't encourage me to love myself and I'm on good terms with that — we were not meant to be an Indian Summer. Instead, you taught me to love a city who needs intimacy and careful hands to help direct its next path. I will take that with me instead.

Maybe I never wanted to say "I love you." Maybe I wanted to say "thank you" instead and mistook my gratitude for passion during our period of infatuation.

***

You are the one I unintentionally loved first, you are the aches in the curves of my feet after trekking through Detroit's blistering winter winds, a double-edged sword delivered directly to my doorstep, the first person I look for on every Friday night dance floor — I almost always catch you there.

You are still laughing as you look back at me from the seat of your bike, cruising down our familiar avenues. Your hands are still placed on the base of my neck. You're every late night touch I have conquered, you are my rooted hurt.

Thank you for your magic.

***

I thought I wanted to leave for a while. I remember staring at the Ambassador Bridge from the back of a fogged up car — he and I were almost underneath it — I remember thinking I wasn't cut out for this.

I remember my mom coming to visit and instead of telling her all the things I hated about work I told her I wasn't sure I could handle the city I knew I loved quite yet. It was bucking me. I'd dig my heels in and she'd rise and make me take flight time and time again. I told my mother I was lonely and there hadn't been light for me here lately.

How can I not be ready to love when I know I am capable?

When I was younger — though I'm not old enough to inherently know many of the world's truth quite yet — I believed my most intimate moments would always be with men in a bed. Or in backs of cars. The female relationships I hold close have also developed on mattresses. Holding onto a best friend's hand as you fall asleep listening to the whining chords of her ex-boyfriend's band even though she never liked them anyway, laying next to my mother and combing hair with the same texture as mine and telling her she did okay.

These are the most intimate - holding my hers through hurt men put them through but cannot comprehend. This is intimacy. This is love.

She bucked me but I held on, I laid in my city every night and told her she could trust me, repeating it softly until it became a mumbled chant, a mantra. She eventually gave her elusive permission to stay. I think that is love.

***

***

I ran away from the city I love far too many times during that period of prolonged healing the same way people vacated it for decades - the shameful journey I often talk about disparagingly.

People began fleeing Detroit long before the riots the historians and naysayers seem to pinpoint as our demise. The population peaked in the early 1950s and saw decline from there. The downward arch began quietly at first. I call these people who ran cowards and traitors (living in this city can make you a purist) I joined them unwittingly for awhile.

They were running for no reason other than misplaced resentment and so was I. I did not want to be like them any longer, the people who fled Detroit by giving into these self-induced pressures.

Everytime I left I never found the gritty artistry of Detroit in any other city roads or bridges or waterfronts. I was not aware of the serenity I gained here until I was absent. While exploring cities that did not awaken me from my outward numbness, I grew powerful enough to realize I could survive within these city limits because you had not built them, they existed far before we did and have evolved in unimaginable ways to retain their structure. I will too and this city and I will grow back side-by-side.

I had created the box I forced myself into, I carved my way out and stayed put.

***

***

I finally called a friend, this time from the living room floor:
"I find it hard to wrap my head around the fact that we all don't get to end up with our soulmates."

She said:

"Because "soulmates" can be narcissistic, ending up with a person who has your core doesn't equate to goodness. They don't always bring out the best in you. In fact, they may eradicate the most fantastic things as you decide their similar traits are more powerful and more worthy of staying than your own.

Sometimes we end up with the person who shows us goodness, instead of the person who shows us everything else, because we must truly be good before we can truly be in love."

***

***

I am always picking the strangest ways to say goodbye:
"You don't belong in this lifetime, love, but let us try the next."

***

I let you enter again (a few times) about a year after we officially parted ways - when we ran into each other at bars and the couple times you called me from the laundromat next to my apartment. When I would join you there to help fold socks, we both knew we were returning to my bed once the dryer cycle was complete.

And in these few hours that transported us to honeymoon feelings, we'd delve back into the intimate habits we had mastered just for an hour, or the night.

When your head was on my pillow I couldn't visualize you yelling at me.
Me snapping back, us pushing away.

Instead we replaced it with pushing hair back from each other's faces, lying face down across the other's back, picking food out of each other's teeth, pulling one another's loose lips into a smile while trying not to giggle. But when you would fall asleep with your back toward me I'd glare at the rosacea that encased the back of your neck.

It takes a certain kind of power to resuscitate something everyone tells you is expired.
Maybe with places that's useful, maybe with people it isn't.

How do you nurture something that has no intention of being tamed? It leaves your hands dirty. It makes you look at your heart outside of your chest cavity, as you hold it in a reached out hand. It will leave you questioning whether this one-sided effort is worth it at all. It will tell you it doesn't need you when it is on its back.

People and places who are on their last leg are stubborn like that. They are precious, they are fickle.

Is it about tender touch or picking it up from the root?
There's no easy way out. You have to try both.

Like I attempted to do for you.
Like I try to do every day for this city.

Because, that is how you love a wildflower.

***

***

I sat up, gazing across the building tops spanning eastward from my apartment parking lot. A mix of sirens on the freeway and the small glaciers that had formed on the side of my building slipping down the creases of brick echoed in the bedroom.

I looked down at you,
"It's raining."
"It's melting, babe." You turned over and let the inside of my leg go, but not before kissing my knee.

An hour later was our closer in a bed -
"There were some points where I was close to saying it. That I loved you."
"I tried waiting for that," I said.
"I know. It was late."

An hour after that, you were rising from our overnight ruins quickly and stuffing your shoes onto the wrong feet, the tongues askew, uncomfortably tucked inside. As you tripped out the way we came in, you kissed my neck instead of my knee.

My knee.
My knee.
My knee.

***

71

***

I sleep on four different men's mattresses now.
Sometimes on Tuesdays around dawn, sometimes all day on Sundays.

I sit on their naked backs, rubbing out knots in their shoulders with the curves of my thumbs; as they lay face down they tell me they miss their mothers because she's cross-country now and how their fathers who still reside in the suburban houses they grew up in used to hit them with belts in the garage. But (they assure me, really) they are fine now.

I sit on their backs, kneading their muscles into straighter lines, listening to their muffled prayers for these old beasts to unhook from the space near their spines.

All the tattoos I have, that bled when they were given, are from the hands of men who I've slept with — we rent out the spaces next to us in bed to those who possess small semblances of the people we're hoping will come back.

I mold their backs into smooth lines and when I speak, they sit faceup.

When I ask, they can all tell me they do not love me.

***

I'm drunk, I'm driving.
I know I shouldn't be. I should be seventeen again and put my keys in a bowl somewhere.

He's in the passenger seat of the aging car I bought after saving up mountains of pennies and minimum-wage paychecks. The boy I lost my virginity to also sat there — same graying seat, different palm on my leg — as we escaped to the freshwater coastline to touch for the first time. You spent ample time in that seat too.

Blonde's playing from the warped car speakers and he makes a comment that he loves this voice too. Is he playing into me? If he is, I do not ask him to try and identify our shared interests further. Instead, I wrap my hand around the one he has placed on the inside of my thigh and squeeze, tight.

He takes this as a lucky sign from God to move closer (not just my palpable air of desperation) and by the time I pull into his driveway his mouth has been turning my neck purple for several blocks. He can't wait.

We slam car doors and meet at the trunk and without warning, he pulls me on top of him on the cold sidewalk crushing the weeds that fill burgeoning cracks and the tiny helicopter leaves that had begun falling the week before. I sat on top and he unzipped himself. The house across the street had a dim lamp glowing in the front window. I heard someone trying to start their car down the street, his breathing gets harder and drowns out everything when I lean my head down to be closer to his airway. We stayed there awhile.

I had been high for so long,
I had to learn whether the ground felt the same.

***

I didn't learn my father was a light sleeper
Until it was too late.

He must have heard
Every little thing I did.

***

Men after you kept telling me what I needed.

Like true gentlemen, they excused themselves upfront for their future actions. Whether they were informing me I needed their dick in my mouth or clarifying on the first night we spent together I was going to need more attention than they could give (or were willing to give me.)

"You need someone who's ready for this type of relationship."
"I have bigger projects to focus on, and you don't want me to be half-committed, do you?"
"I don't date because of her, but you can still come over tonight."

And, I am sorry, I let them.

I was raised by a woman who made it clear from the jump that women are the superior sex - a woman who told me marriage is antiquated and we should never sign ourselves over if what we're feeling doesn't move us. For better or for absolute rock bottom, we all become products of our mothers' hearts.

After twenty-five years of marriage, my parents still have secrets they hold tightly — I know because my mother told me some of hers.

How close do we ever really get to the people who sleep in our beds even when their heat is so close that it consumes us? The most staggering catch-22 overtook me frequently, I started strong with every new man and ended punished by uncertainty, thinking their inability to love was instead a weakness of mine.

It was easier for them to tell me what they couldn't do rather than telling them what I wanted.

***

***

This is around the time where the fragility and care surrounding my sexuality was disregarded - that kind of care women are supposed to hold on to with a tight grip and let spiral into a freefall whenever we're presented with a sexual proposal.

I let people tug my hair out the same way I do when I'm panicking, I let them deep inside me with no barrier. I didn't care. I let my body tear open from the ribcage as men searched for the heart inside of me, crawling between the organs I still needed.

I do not think my sexuality is sacred, or something to be kept stored away, because my body holds immeasurable power. Our sex is used against us as our martyr rather than being acknowledged as our natural pedestal. I didn't find myself recognizing the worth of my sex until I was gently telling you where to go and what to do underneath the covers. I was bionic when you were with me, you were the first to acknowledge the sanctity of the curves in my figure with your touches and exalted breathes against the dip between my ribs and hips.

I lost this when you left. I searched for this pleasure on top of many bedsprings, letting the feeling of being turned around and taken happen more and more often. I faltered and assumed my dominance and strength had been imagined. My path to retracing my steps and discovering my innate magic once again came from nights of evolving into someone who takes control rather than letting people not-so-gently enter me. It takes practice. It's made up of missteps.

Rediscovering your value after it has left for a time is not a failure.

That's beauty.
That's grace.
That's love.

***

We found each other when we were still in the process of growing up.

Twenty-two and twenty-four are not the right times to commit to the unrequited — while we are trying to pay rent on salaries our universities guaranteed would sustain us, plagued with adult concerns we had been warned about but brushed off by burning the student loan bills in bonfires in your backyard.

A whole lot of privilege forced into a billow of smoke.

We entered a grown-up relationship we were too naive to manage because these are all new firsts but definitely not lasts. For our generation, big love is contained to our tiny apartments.

When I said I wanted to tell you "thank you" earlier, I forgot to say this -

Thank you for providing me with the notion that growing up is a transformation rather than something metastasizing.
Thank you for still needing me in the morning.
Thank you, thank you, thank you.

I'm older now and I'm better. I miss you.

***

Voicemails were the most venomous things I left you for awhile:

March: *"Am I hotter to you like this? Are lines the only thing you want to see me put in my body? Do you think it'll help even me out? Is it a turn-on for you to find out when I stopped taking the pills I immediately started to relive your smell and sounds?"*

July: *"You said I was sexy. You said I was more exciting this way. This is the brain you loved, touched, enhanced and left. But you didn't create this, I just called because you should know you're not my source."*

September: *"I'm getting everything under control, for good this time. I meant to tell you when I saw you out, but I didn't want to put a damper on your night. Hope you didn't stay out too late...I always have coffee here if you need it. I'm thinking things would have been nicer this way."*

***

I received only one voicemail from you after we slept together for the final time. Just a simple string of words, no goodbye.

Tuesday, 6:20 a.m.:

"In the mornings, I miss looking at that church — you know, the one without the steeple bells — across from your old place."

***

***

Yesterday a guy at the bar tried to pick me up by telling me I have "sad eyes"
he'd like to make better.
I laughed and wondered if that made a difference.

I don't think humans have yet discovered a way to kiss their own forehead wrinkles,
or pull themselves across the mattress at midnight for another round,
but I have found a steadiness.
I burned the journal with the lovely notes
I wrote about you - the select few scribblings I let you read,
after you pleaded for a brief look inside.
I stood over the lumber I had thrown together
and inhaled the smoke from that fire,
knowing it was the last time I would allow myself to breathe you in.

My shower flitted from cold to warm
and then back to cold this morning.
I laughed to myself because it was reminiscent of you
and I wonder if that made a difference.

***

***

The first man who loved me after you is wild and gentle. His hair hangs past his chest and sometimes he bathes with a garden hose because his shower only turns on when the pipes in his aging house feel generous. He turns the hose around when he's done and gives the flowerbeds and seedlings around him a good spray.

He is thoughtful. He understands on some days I want to kiss his face in every space I can land my mouth on. He knows other times it is harder for me to keep the goodbye letters in their envelopes instead of tossing them out the window of the getaway car I have eternally idling. We get naked and eat mangos in his breakfast nook, we suck the drizzling juice from each other's chests.

I do not think it's settling when you've found someone who appreciates the Jekyll and Hyde of you and not just the side of your face that catches the sun.

On an incredibly bland May day, peace touched my shoulder and blew through my golden-again hair and I only thought twice.

***

He's going to fuck me.

He says what we do isn't fucking.The difference here, he says, is I'm supposed to look directly at him this time. Although, I looked at you — you still said "fuck."

Here, I'm supposed to lean in to his palms. I'm a participant instead of a "pussy."

I guess here I am a "decision-maker," a "teller," a sweat and a taste that is "appreciated," a voice that is loud, and louder, and louder. I drown him out. His hand is not over my mouth and I'm not biting it like yours. And his. And his. And his.

His voice is deeper than yours and it bounces from the dark corners to the hallway parallelogram — but he can be quiet.

You were never silenced - you talked and whispered and shouted and those noises never bounced away from us.
I clung to and worked to embody every single word.

***

***

The old lady who lived in the apartment next to me, who loved to talk to you in the hall, got a new dog before I moved. At least it sounded like it, the pitch of the chorus through the wall changed. I heard it on my last night in that room.

To me, she was a manifestation of something extraordinary; even as you grow older, you are able to make changes and additions to the collection of things you love.

My favorite moments in this life will always occur right before a reassemble.

They are my bubbling orbs of breath let go while under the surface of freshwater that has always surrounded me after I decide I can't stay under much longer. They are noticing the potted plant, swinging in the kind of wind only magical Michigan springs can conjure, on the patio of a home on the east side that has come back to life after many hands worked to salvage its foundation.

My most coveted moments will always occur after days of asking myself "how do I reconstruct this?"

Here's how I rebuild: I fill the rips to my body to the brim with fuchsia petals from those swinging plants, lanterns attached to thin strands of yarn I could tie from fingertip to fingertip if I wanted to, and moths that are always looking for their next lit-up home and all the other pretty, significant things and people and ideas I am able to save and place in myself and give homes to and watch prosper.

***

I hope you get to meet me now. I am resurrected - alive and at odds with the girl who is in the dearest moments you also relive every so often.

I have not forced any interaction with you, my catalyst. You told me I'd be ready for life one of these days. You touched months-old crippled leaves on my coffee table and said "you can't keep a ficus alive, but man, you have enough life in that damn body."

Your ghost and its statements are permanent — as easy to fall victim to as your lustrous, all-consuming presence. And the dreams about simple in-and-outs of breath reverberating back to me from the cove of your chest without teeing off a sense of madness are what prove to me I'm anew.

The girl who clung to the decayed is dead and you chose absence from me too — they died together and that makes two.

***

***

I grabbed the sunflower pin out of a box marked "everything two dollars" at a vintage shop on the west side. The center ceramic pistil was hanging off slightly — I rushed home to repair it with the super glue I kept in the bottom junk drawer among screwdrivers and used birthday candles and other forgotten items we *need*. The petals had chipped to the white undercoat, with rings of slight yellow framing the edges.

It was a new summer — I was awake again — I fastened my flower to the jean jacket I wore most. She sat on a faded lapel just above the left breast and attracted attention there; I didn't switch its position even once this became apparent after just a few wears.

You caught me leaving a new cafe. You were there with your father and I felt now would be an inappropriate moment to introduce myself after I thought "how do I introduce myself?"

We waved with both hands from a distance, we were close enough to maybe yell words or possibly teach each other any lesson in lip-reading, but we were not close enough to reach out.

"How are you?" I mouthed.
"That's a nice flower," you said.

***

***

A word to my fellow re-bloomers -

I have not found the time I put into getting to know myself without him,
(and being re-diagnosed,
and treated with loving hands who offered themselves up on their own,
and finding empty fields and swing sets with just one seat across my city,
and concluding if you are only happy with one other person it is not right and it is not good,
and loving beautiful men from afar with no intention of ever saying a word)
before I gave myself up to anyone again, wasn't worth it.

***

What I am able to think *now*,
if you had told me you were not going to settle in our space *then*:

If you are thinking about leaving, you should. Another woman will love you the same way I did and her touch may be softer and her hair may be more tame — except I'm sure you will pick someone with a head wilder than mine, I know — and it will feel certain. Your jokes will land and she will want to get in the truck and drive to your favorite neighborhood too. She may not point out the same houses I did, but those that she picks will be intricate and magnificent nonetheless.

She will.

She will let you bask in the hurt of parents parting ways — the kind that sticks forever — and wanting to be somewhere other than here and she will use her lips to stop those tears when you say you miss your mother. She will do it better than I could. She will say she doesn't want to get married either, "because how could you ever willingly pass that kind of pain onto another generation, you know?" She'll sit on that tattered oriental rug on your back porch.

She will help you move when you need to bop around houses to avoid complacency the way you do. She'll also love when you wake her up on fall dawns with the sound of the kettle exhaling on the stove - tea brewing.

If you are thinking about leaving, go.

I will not be the mother of your children,
but you will make sure she also has daisies in her hair.

Tomorrow will be better.
Next year you will be freer than you are now.
She will do these things for you,
I am certain, she will.

***

***

You no longer sit cross-legged, forehead to mine.
You've etched yourself into a man of routine,
But I still know it's you,
my brilliant machine.

***

***

Running into you now does not elicit the uncontrollable breathing and flinches I tried to contain and at first begged to medicate away. We hadn't planned to meet when I first saw you seven months after you told me we had become mundane. But, it's like you knew I was coming before I stepped into our places — we were supposed to meet on this planet so coming upon one another in bookstores or narrow alleyways on Sunday mornings is not happenstance but rather it is divine.

Our part of Detroit has always felt small.

But, how did your eyes take on that color that particular morning? I searched for "shades of purple" after I left and found the one that matches you most - it's mauve.

The look they gave still shakes me.

That is how you look at the one who has been featured in your past lives.
That is the look you give people who brushed your hand the first day you met and you didn't back away because it already felt like you had touched me, shocked me, shot me and I had dreamt this all before.

Sometimes when I see you in daylight now, I am still shocked we ever escaped our 4 a.m.

It all feels cosmic, baby.
You deserve a small worship.

***

About the author:

Chloe Camille Seymour is a Detroit-based writer. A lifelong Michigander, she has inevitably become a diehard Lions fan (don't hold that against her) and an advocate for positive narratives in Detroit.

A believer in "girl power, baby" ever since the Spice Girls jumped off their tour bus and shouted it loud and proud, Chloe is enticed by opportunities to tell female-led stories. Also a blind devotee to the idea of love, she is a sucker for any kind of love story revolving around people, places and pop music icons.

She can be reached at chloecamillewrites.com.

Made in the USA
Lexington, KY
17 September 2018